The Caretaker's Cottage Library

The Hidden Journals
Mystery, Macabre and More

Andrea Dean Van Scoyoc

~**Foreword:**~

A collection of somber and even...macabre tales, based on my love of the strange and unusual, I hope this book brings you as much enjoyment in reading it, as it did me in the writing of it.

My imagination is a wild and strange place, even frightening for some to enter, but one thing remains certain...

If it creeps in the fog or appears at Midnight, whether it crawls in gloom or hides at dawn's first light, you'll find me reading it or writing about it.

Bugs and Hisses,

Andrea

~Table of Content~

Flowers By The Window

The vases lined up on the window sill in the library, dying flowers in them all.

She gazed intently at the dried, dropping petals and the withered, brown foliage.

A voice broke her troubled, wandering mind.

"That's us, you know."

"How so?"

Hasilyn turned to see her cousin, Rena, standing behind her. She and Rena had never been close. Glum, morose and just plain...weird...Hasilyn had never had any use for her mother's sister's only child. But...deaths in the family tended to bring everyone together, no matter how much their company was dreaded.

Rena smirked. Hasilyn got the strange feeling that whatever Rena was going to say, it was going to be creepy. She thrived on that.

"We were once fresh, young and beautiful too. We still are. But one day, we won't be. We'll wither, we'll fade and we'll eventually die.

Isn't it strange that something so simple, something we really don't think about, can open our eyes to such a profound connection to our own lives?"

Hasilyn turned back to the vases of flowers. The afternoon sun filtered through the window, giving the solemn scene an eerie glow; almost like a halo settling around the room.

It had been one month since Great Aunt Jiselle's funeral and the flowers seemed to be drained... almost as her favorite Great Aunt's life had drained and then been buried away.

As much as Rena continued to creep her out during their lives, on that particular day, Hasilyn developed a newfound appreciation for her cousin's morose outlook.

She had the type of realistic relationship with the macabre that most chose to ignore...

The Demon Of The Moor

One of the many heirlooms I have left over from the grand old days of the Estate, is my Great Grandmother's journal.

Her name was Lady Ann DeKay and I've shared some of her previous pennings.
She was quite the poet, author, entertainer, and creative soul and I am so fortunate to have so much of her to share with you.
It almost didn't turn out that way.
When she died, in a fit of rage, one of her children destroyed the many trunks of music that had been left to *her*. Pages and pages of handwritten sheet music with accompanying lyrics.
That woman was my Grandmother's sister, Harlen. She thought she deserved more.
My Grandmother told me that Lady Ann's music was beautiful and they used to spend hours around the piano, listening to her play and singing the songs she'd written.

Sometimes, when I walk the Estate, late at night, I can hear the faint refrains of tragically beautiful piano music and I somehow feel closer to that grand old Lady.

Luckily, the journal, filled with Ann's hauntingly chilling but darkly romantic prose, went to my Grandmother. Unlike her greedy sister, my Grandmother held that journal above all she ever owned and knowing that I possessed that same sentimentality and appreciation, left it to me.

Her diary is one of my most treasured possessions.

I've been reading an entry from 1915. It appears that, at one time, the Estate was smaller than it is now and Lady Ann and Lord Blackledge (my great Grandfather) had neighbors!

This is from October 29th...just in time for All Hallow's Eve. My Grandmother always loved a good ghost story.

Now I know where she got it from. It appears that Lady Ann was quite the story collector herself...in addition to writing them.

Here is the entry, word-for-word...
I hope you enjoy it as much as I have...

*From The Diary of Lady Ann DeKay
October 29, 1915...*

My neighbor, Lina, whom I'm quite fond of, is Irish. She's very old (though she will never say just *how* old!) widowed, with no children and treats Blackie and I as her own. She says she's leaving us everything (including her house and land. An impressive lot indeed!) when she passes.
Whether or not she does, is of no concern to me and certainly not to Blackie. We both simply love her for her light, her wisdom and her kindness.
She's absolutely fascinating and tells the most interesting tales. This one such tale, she says, was passed down by her mother, who heard it from *her* mother.
She relayed it to me, exactly as it was passed down to her, which I thoroughly enjoyed.
Being a poet myself, this really struck me and I committed it to memory.

I added the introduction and footnote, for my own special touch.

May she always live on in this entry...

I chatted over the fence today with Lina who lives next door.

She told me an interesting story about a man who lived on the moor.

The man was a drunkard, wretched and mean,

He lied and stole and cheated in between.

No one would challenge him and his fists of stone.

For, one hit could shatter the strongest bone.

He blasphemed his Creator, and he liked it that way,

But all of that changed on one cloudy cold day.

While on his way home, the sun dipped low,

Angry at lost time, he had further to go.
To cut across the bog was the quickest way,
He'd never heeded what others had to say.

He'd heard the tales about what lived in the night,
A demon of old that held the bog tight.
"The marsh will swallow any caught after dark,
Like water on a fire, drowning every last spark."
The old man scoffed, liquid courage in his veins,
Little did he know, he'd never be seen again.
The last anyone saw in the pale waning light,
He set off across the moor and disappeared out of sight.
In the dark, screams were heard, distant and shrill,
The demon had claimed, yet another kill.
And that was the end of old Dugan McShea,
His awful ways ended on that cold winter's day.
When the story was over, I laughed...

"Lina...did it *really* happen that way?"
Lina smiled and winked,
"My Granny remembered that night 'til her final dying day."

The Dead Man's Party

The book's crumbling pages belied the mystery inside. Secrets, gossip and even murder.

A carefully chronicled diary, few in pages but ripe with intrigue; a tale of seven guests and a weekend soiree at a beautiful, Gothic estate.

According to what information managed to survive, only one reveler would make it out alive and no one had ever been able to solve the crime.

If there had been a survivor, he or she had never come forward.

The local police were wholly unequipped to deal with such a baffling case. Were they paid off, or were they simply inept? Judging by the guest list, money would *not* have been in short supply, so it was possible.

In high society, money had always spoken louder than justice.

The book spent time in a leaky attic in a rotting trunk, then moved to and later found in... the basement of an abandoned home.

By the time the decrepit tome made it to the museum, some one hundred years later, only the following poem and red and black invitation, wrapped in an old newspaper clipping dated 1880, survived.

They were found in an envelope, wrapped in leather, in between the faded and crumbling pages of what was left of the diary.

"Seven guests at a lavish estate. Do everyone a favor and don't be late!

Murder and mystery will claim all but one, a stab, a shot or maybe a fall...and you're done!

There's a lake for swimming and a horse to ride. You won't be safe so don't bother to hide.

If those won't please, you're not left out, here's some fun, without a doubt...

The garden is bliss and as beautiful as dawn, with a poisonous twist, you won't last long.

For the studious among you, the library awaits, just pass through the curtains and wrought iron gate.

The fireplace stays lit and the books are all rare, but mind what you read and choose with care.

Drinks will flow, only the finest wine, the gluttony might kill you, it'll be so divine. Are you hungry? The kitchen will serve only the finest cuisine, veggies and cakes and meat oh-so lean.

At the end of the day when you're good and tired, when your energy has waned and long since expired, a private bedroom awaits...with a four-poster bed...

But don't expect much rest...because by dawn, six of the seven of you will be long since...DEAD!"

Just as the poem said, on Monday morning, six illustrious, if not scandalous and controversial members of the community, were found dead in their guest beds at the estate.
The causes of death were varied and coincided with the poem. It seemed that the *only* deathly scenario left untouched...was the library, where according to legend, the diary was found. Strangely enough, the families were relieved, if not happy, to be rid of the "blights" on their family name, so the investigation was not seriously pursued, even though some very interesting questions lingered.

The first and most pressing question was...
How did the killer obtain the keys to the Estate?

Originally known as the, "Landham Estate," it was built by Captain Jessup Archlyn Landham, a well respected sea captain (and often privateer...though people tended to overlook that as his family was so well liked and respected) in 1758.

All was well until around 1840 when the family name and fortune began to founder. By 1880, the once illustrious and very wealthy Landham family had fallen to ruin with the descendants of Jessup Landham wiping out everything their noted ancestor had worked for.

The descendants that *had* wanted to save the family home had neither the means, nor the money needed to continue its upkeep, let alone to restore it, so the glorious abode was lost to property taxes numbering in the tens of thousands.

Seized, auctioned off and sold again and again, it finally fell into disuse and abandonment...and by 1880, ultimately decaying into a crumbling hulk of stone.

There was no owner. So, again the question begged...*how* did anyone get the keys to the estate?

Who'd had the party and... *what* was the goal of killing off the black sheep from upper society's key families?

No one would ever know.

The ancient record saved from almost complete ruin...the twisted account of a weekend party gone horribly wrong, the only proven survivor.

The Garden of Death

From a dream I came to this place,
A garden of deadly delights,
A busy place of sickening smells,
And a nightmare of sorrow and sight,

Shadowed souls come with treacherous goals,
Such stories do they tell,
Tales of murder and mysteries unsolved,
Using poisons they know so well...

She remembered reading that poem during her childhood. It had often been used in olden days to frighten naughty children into behaving.
Based on old folklore from the nineteen hundreds it was the product of a murderous student who took revenge on his classmates by poisoning them at a school picnic, his justification being their cruel and incessant teasing.

He ran away and was never caught.

Now, though it had lost any power it once had, she still found the legend striking. It was the foreword in a book based on that long forgotten murder in her hometown. She'd immediately become obsessed with the knowledge of ancient apothecary...specifically...poisons, the first time she found the heavy, hardbound book on a back shelf in the corner of the library.

Just one copy.

The publisher had been a local newspaper man back in the day and since the publisher had *long* gone out of business, the book became as forgotten almost, as the murder.

The book was a treasure...even if she were the only one to appreciate it.

It had never been required reading at school, (not even her history teacher was interested! All he cared about was the Renaissance era it seemed, not the small town goings on of "Anywhere USA,") but she checked it out every chance she got. She'd even considered stealing it. She was the only one who ever checked it out, so who would even notice; except those who knew of her love for the antique tome...

The librarians.

They grimaced at her "morbidity" and her teacher rolled her eyes at her when she chose to do a book report on the ancient flowers of death responsible for the rash of grisly crime.

Where had her fondness for poisoning and murder mystery come from?

She couldn't answer that, nor did she try. She just found deadly plants interesting. She planned to be a murder mystery author when she graduated High School, so as far as she was concerned, this was simply research...

That and she also had a deep desire to know more about the young man who'd done the killings. Oh, there had been debates, wringing of hands, blame and heated arguments about "horrible children" and what failure their parents had been.

On the other hand, the parents of the young man eventually left town, as they were targeted for death, their home vandalized and the family grocery store burned to the ground.

It was all sordid, it was all gripping...it was all in the book. One name kept popping up as the catalyst for the young man's murderous idea...Tameraine Chelting.

Odd at best, he was an eccentric, an English immigrant; some said, physician and some said, mad man.

He'd treated many people who didn't have the money for conventional medical treatment. Supposedly, he'd saved many lives. If he had been innocent as he always claimed of influencing or even helping the young lad, no wonder he left town! Many blamed him for so freely sharing his knowledge with anyone who wished to learn.

She was glad she lived in modern times. Everyone thought she was weird, that her interest in an all but forgotten mystery that paled in comparison to modern serial killing sprees, was stupid and a waste of time.

Not that she cared what others thought of her, but imagine if she'd lived back then! She too would have been a target. She shuddered at the possibility.

She looked at the plants surrounding her. She'd heard the stories of people getting sick, even vomiting and some passing out if they stayed around them for too long.

A park employee made sure to limit guest exposure.

She hoped her gas mask would be enough to help her spend a little more time than a few minutes, making her notes. The ticket lady snickered at her as she walked in. She supposed she did look like something out of a zombie apocalypse movie. She dreamed as she walked...wondering if the killer had walked this same path, looked at the same flowers, made the same notes.

She read the names of some of the highlighted plants. Each month new "killer plants" were featured. "Belladonna, Monksbane, Angel's Trumpet, Corpse Flower and Oleander." She'd done enough research to know that Oleander grew rampantly in Florida. They planted it on the side of the road and in medians as decoration, according to someone she chatted with online. The gal had also told her the local urban legend about a group of nine kids on a beach by something called the "Courtney-Campbell Causeway," burning Oleander plants on a bonfire while they hung out partying and the next morning, they were all found dead; dead from the poison smoke from the flowers and wood.

"Fascinating," she muttered, "that something so pretty and delicate looking could be so deadly."

The local authorities, while mostly dismissing the mystery of, "The Garden of Death," as uninteresting history, didn't wish for a repeat of such an awful event from the town's distant past. About a decade ago, another angry, outcast and bullied student tried to copycat the mass killing.

Visitors were carefully watched now and video cameras were everywhere

But...unlike the original killer, *that* young man had been caught in rapid time.

"Hemlock," she muttered. As old as time itself, almost, this plant had been mentioned many times in the book.

She made notes as she walked around. Between her exhaustive research at the local library on the case, her extensive research at the historical society on the town's early inhabitants and even tracing the killer's assumed steps before the murders, she was sure she'd eventually at least shed some light on the morgue-cool mystery.

She bit her bottom lip. To most it probably didn't seem like such a mystery, but to her, it was almost a journey she felt she had to undertake.

26

Schools a long time ago were strict weren't they? When was the young man bullied? Was it before school? During school? After school? If during school, why was it allowed?

In the modern world, school was almost dog-eat-dog; you'd better be able to take care of yourself because school authorities were more concerned about the rights of the bullies than the bullied.
But, though young at the time, she remembered her Grandmother telling her stories of how school was back in *her* day and how *her* teacher liked to use a ruler on rowdy kids and how often she saw the boys yanked up by their ears, for misbehaving.
Didn't anyone see the whole awful event...coming? *Anyone*?

Her eyes drifted back up to the grotesque Corpse Plant before her.
What a book report this would be and she was certain...would be just the first step to a grand career as an author whose name would go down in murder mystery history.

NEVER SATISFIED

"Don't touch me like that!"

Her voice was so irritating to him. She never stopped. It was always, "I don't want to go there," or, "You're such a jerk!" Today, she was really on his last nerve. Why was it none of the other guys had to put up with a yammering woman? Why him? What had he done that he deserved...her?

Finally, enough of her shrill harping, he turned around and looked at her. She stared blankly at him, which was typical. "Look, I don't know what you expected. If you don't like how you're treated, maybe you shouldn't have willed yourself to a body farm after your death"!

He shrank back and looked around. What would people think if they caught him talking to rotting corpses?

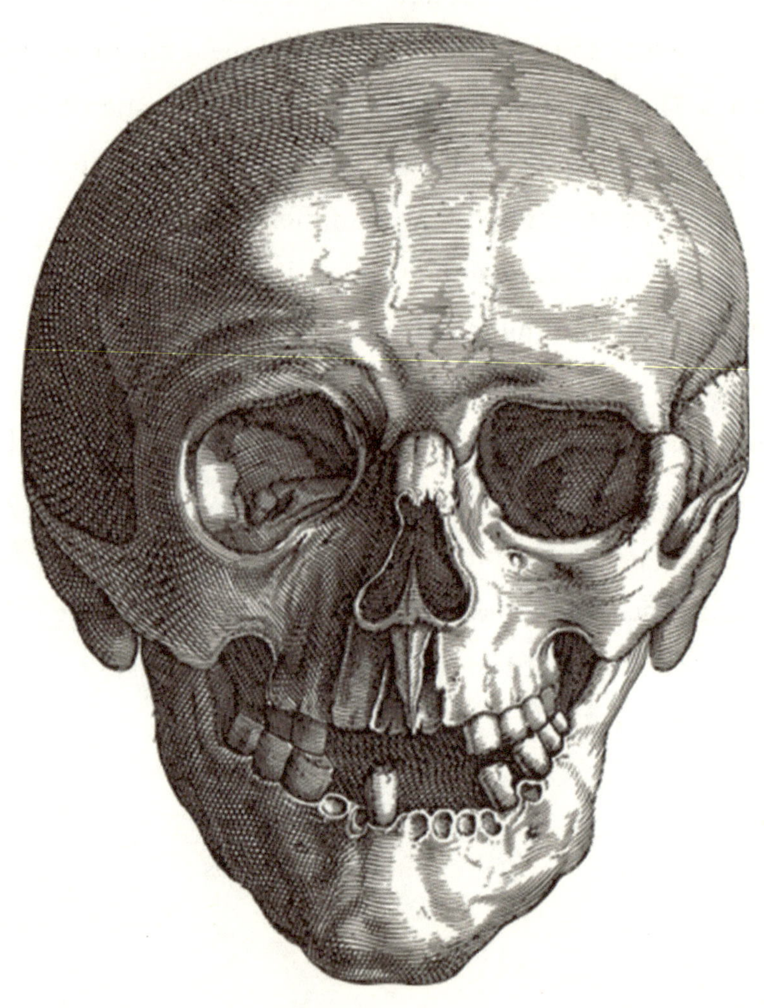

The Harbinger

The Last Day...

...For men shall be lovers of their own selves, covetous, boasters, proud, blasphemers, disobedient to parents, unthankful, unholy, without natural affection, trucebreakers, false accusers, incontinent, fierce, despisers, of those that are good... **2 Timothy 3:1-9**

As I sit here and look down over the hustle and bustle of this thriving city and what used to be a beautiful oasis; before development took it from nature and handed it to you, I'm both troubled and giddy by how things really got to be *this* bad.

Though many omens, stories and a book even foretold this day, I *honestly* never thought I'd see it happen.

While I can't say that I had *faith* in you fleshers to straighten up your acts, I misjudged the common sense I believed you to have. I truly expected you to wake up and see what you were squandering away.

I'm not used to being wrong and *was I ever!*

With each new generation that sprang up from the decay of the previous one, I saw more and more waste, self-centeredness, entitlement and greed became like a cancer, consuming everyone that got even a taste of anything they craved.

All of these horrific flaws; the mistake of what it means to be nothing more than an experiment gone terribly wrong in the form of you Fleshers - humans - were the shadowed whispers of what was to come.

Even the simple act of love, was replaced with loathing; though I will admit that leading up to this day, there wasn't much reason to love any of you and I can't say that I really remember a time that *any* of you were worthy of love. A good kick, maybe...death, sickness...that I can agree with, but love?

Not for a long time.

You Fleshers have done nothing but play victim since the Creator made the mistake of forming Adam from the dust. It could be no other way - you were destined to fall by and by nothing more than your own doings.

Ironically, you Fleshers have a saying... 'Give a person enough rope and they'll hang themselves.' Prophetic words indeed...

Reminiscing...

At first you weren't so bad. You were manageable, you were...*controllable*...and you minded, like good pets should.

But as your intelligence and curiosity grew and I suppose I should mention, as you became lazier, I realized that you are hopeless...as did the others.

You are children, simpering, whimpering, pathetic little children and if things don't go your way, you pout, cause trouble and stamp your feet like the spoiled drama queens you all dish about in your pathetic lives; gobbling up each and every morsel of dirt you can find.

It might not surprise you to hear that we do the same...only our dirt dishing comes at *your* expense. You're unruly brats...and that trait – in all of you - has simply gotten worse. From the day you're born you are treated like the royalty you are not, *nor will you ever be.*

I guess that brings me to the arrogance so many of you display on a daily basis.

Never in my existence, which spans far longer than your feeble minds (for all the intelligence you *think* you have) can comprehend, have I seen such self-delusion and visions of grandeur.

I should include in this assessment as well, the rash entitlement you all *think* you deserve. It's laughable and you are all the more pathetic for it. What's so sad is that you are the only ones who can't see it.

Those of us, privy to the oncoming war that is brewing in every plane of existence (no matter the side we follow,) enjoy a good laugh at your expenses; one of the few commonalities we *all* share.

No matter which side you Fleshers follow and even if you follow no side, we laugh at you, because you think you have a good idea of what life is all about. You honestly think you have it all figured out and if you are humble enough to *not* think so, you still think that you have a good idea.

The Downfall...

You couldn't be further from the truth.

Did you actually think that many (if any) of us had hope for you? We didn't, believe me.

While I never *really* thought He'd have the balls to go through with it, I also hoped He would.

I have no loyalty to Him or anyone else...I'm simply here to do a job and you cannot imagine how long an eternity is, when waiting to see you Fleshers get what you deserve.

I can't say that I was *always* so cynical, but looking back, it's been a *long* time in coming. You have stripped me of every vestige of hope.

There have been times that I saw random acts of kindness, empathy, compassion and even selflessness...people giving their lives for each other and for causes, goals and dreams bigger than them.

But it didn't take long to see those same gallant actions overshadowed by your implicit need for validation, your drama, game-playing and woefully sick need for attention – no matter what you have to do, or who you have to hurt, to get it.

After a lifetime of stops and starts on an adventure that could have been a glorious one - only to be let down again and again - I washed my hands of you and began to simply wait to be called to do my duty. In my heart I knew that you would never be...*could* never be what He thought you'd be.

Your god is a petulant child refusing to share toys with any other, a foolhardy teenager speeding through existence in a fancy car that He can't control. Now that He's seen what a joke you've made of yourselves (not to mention Him) His embarrassment can't do anything else, but prompt the orchestration of your destruction.

That and He's losing the bet...

He thought that all you Fleshers would actually follow Him and to His credit, many of you do. All the more sad for you, because even in the apocryphal and blind devotion so many of you sheep show for Him, there simply aren't enough of you and He's losing.

This humiliation He can't allow and so you all must go.

Duty...

That book that so many of you have put such misguided faith in, never speaks of me and that's fine.

I'm used to being hidden away in secrecy.

No one wants to admit I exist...well, some do, but they don't have the power to summon me. I am the, 'ace in the hole,' as you Fleshers like to say, and I can't wake until summoned.

That time has come and I have a job to do.

So here I sit only a moment more, before I take my walk through this city. I have many more to visit after this one, so I really can dally no longer.

I will say this in parting though...you Fleshers really turned a beautiful haven into a sewer. I'll also say that it's my pleasure to reward your acts of wanton...well, everything I've mentioned...as it wasn't just _one_ of those flaws that could cause _Him_ to give up on you, as well... with exactly what you deserve.

I relish the thought, I eagerly await each order and I revel in the suffering I bring to _all_ of you.

You had your chance...too bad you didn't know how to treasure, instead of trash it.

The Reef

The story began long ago with two young people and the Sea,
A fated love that fell to woe and was never meant to be.
The journey was just a quick jaunt out and return before the
night,
The wind was blustery, the fog was thick and rain blocked all
sight.

The shore was close, they'd not far to go, by the moon they were almost there,
Many kisses and dreams awaited, on that secluded island they'd share.
The waves they crashed like walls of sorrow and lightning burned the sky,
How could such a happy couple know that they were about to die?
With a shudder, the boat lurched and crashed atop the craggy reef,
Throwing the lovers overboard and trapping them underneath.
The tale's still told to this day of lovers on the shore,
When storms brew in the night, lost forevermore.
So beware the "Lover's Strait,: as it's come to be known,
Two young people standing on a reef, together...but eternally alone...

The Voice

Chapter One
Introduction

"Are you ready, my sweet?"

Norelle Federiconi started to speak, but a raised hand caused her to recoil. She knew all too well what that gesture meant.

"Don't even think about it, slag. Just nod."

She dropped her head, her eyes welling like they always did when he was so mean to her. She couldn't help it. All she wished for was a kind word, a truly kind word from Franco.

Tears spilled down her cheeks. She hadn't asked to be this way…or maybe she had. Still, Franco didn't have to be so cruel.

Didn't he deserve to be punished for how he treated her? Her face burned.

She felt her body contort awkwardly as he roughly pulled her in front of the tall, oval mirror that seemed to be the only thing elegant in the dingy and ancient dressing room…elegant second only to her.

She gazed at her reflection carefully in the mirror. No matter how many tears she cried, no matter how many beatings she suffered, no matter how many worries caused her sleepless nights, she was still beautiful. Tall and thin with straight shoulders, a flawless complexion and golden shining hair that surrounded her like a white halo, she was a vision.

She blinked and more tears spilled down her cheeks as she felt the brush pull through her hair. Franco always brushed her hair for her before she went on, if he wasn't pulling it in anger. He was actually being gentle...this time.

Her eyes drifted down from her perfect face to her full bosom - the red velvet gown accentuating every curve - all the way down to the red-heeled feet that she couldn't see beneath the rich opulence of the sumptuous fabric.

She was tired.

Her mind drifted back to the early days in her career when she was new to what the roar of the crowd could do for her. She was shy and naïve back then and it took her a while to get used to the crows of "encore, encore," that nearly deafened her. She loved her fame and she loved her fans but it was more than she could keep up with. She never got enough rest it seemed, so Franco began to give her pills - pills to wake her up, pills to put her to sleep, pills to bring her up when she was sad, pills to calm her when she'd been up for three days straight...until she finally had a psychotic episode. The police found her wandering the streets in her nightgown babbling about the devil. Franco had her committed overnight, "for her own good" he assured her, and she was prescribed something that she couldn't pronounce. Franco always made sure that she took her medicine and punished her when she didn't.

With each performance, she knew that the next one had to be better or she would be sorry. Franco counted the throngs of people that showed up to hear "the angel of light" - as she had been dubbed - sing, and if there was even one less person in attendance than the time before, she was beaten. She knew that one day her star would dim and a new and even more talented singer than herself would replace her. What would Franco do to her then?

Chapter Two
Sweet Release

One night she found herself alone when Franco went out to 'tend to business' as he often did. Their house was quiet. The bottle of absinthe, sent to her by an adoring fan, called to her from the ornate, marble topped dresser - a gift shipped to her from a carver in Italy in appreciation for her touring his small city.

She looked over at the newly filled prescription and got up from her bed, gliding silently over to the dresser. Her hand slid around the top of the "liquid sunshine" - her nickname for absinthe - and she caressed it softly. Her life had not been her own since the night Franco found her, singing her heart out in a smoke filled club for barely enough tips to pay for a taxi home.

That night, the night she met Franco, changed her forever.

He took her from her pathetic life of abject poverty to a life of luxury; one that she thought only existed in fairytales. Her life had become a whirlwind of tours, newspaper and magazine articles, television appearances and "more money than God," as Franco liked to say.

She owed him everything...but she hated him too. She'd been touring nonstop for five years and the next five years were booked as well. She couldn't tell him "no," she couldn't refuse *anything* he asked of her because she feared the beatings he could and *would* give her. There was only one way out.

She opened the bottle of medicine and took two pills, chased down by the green fairy in the bottle of liquid sunshine, then two more, followed by more sunshine until the medicine and the green fairy were both gone. She reclined in her soft bed and closed her eyes...she was free.

But she wasn't free...

Chapter Three
A Right Gone Very Wrong

She awoke in a dark room, a bright light shining in her face, blinding her. She slowly sat up, shielding her face from the burning heat that came from...she couldn't discern where. As her eyes adjusted to the artificial illumination and the surrounding gloom, she saw that she was sitting in the *middle* of the brightness, as if she were on stage with a spotlight trained on her. Many times in her career she sang in the spotlight, but she didn't like how *this* attention felt. It frightened her.

She shook her head. She felt woozy.

"Did you really think it would be that easy, Norelle?"

She looked around. Who'd spoken to her? She couldn't see anything, but the voice mocked her.

"Did you really think that the green fairy could rescue you? I found you, you are mine, and you will remain mine forever."

Norelle bowed her head and wept. The voice belonged to someone that she knew all too well...Franco. He stepped to the edge of the circle. She'd always known what he was but had refused to allow herself to think about it...until she couldn't bear her life any longer.

He was the Devil. He was the Devil and her life was Hell.

She'd never known that the Devil could be so handsome, so beguiling, so giving...and so cruel.

From his sharp, expensive suit to his perfectly coiffed hair, to his manicured nails and gleaming white teeth, he looked every bit a dapper gentleman. But what he was, was a beast. He was her savior...and her bane.

She could do nothing but go back to him, she had to.

"Now silly girl, take my hand and come with me, where you belong. You know there will *never* be any escape from me. I have made you rich beyond compare; I have given you more to live for than most people could dream of. I changed you, molded you and made you what you wanted you to be. You owe me, you will owe me for eternity and if you try a stunt like this again, it will be *your* soul that I take."

Norelle's eyes snapped up to look into Franco's black ones.

"Yes, Norelle, you will continue to fulfill the rest of your debt to me, but now I will allow you to *know* as well as see, at your next performance, exactly what it is that you have been doing for me all these years. I have spared you the truth of what your music does to people...until now. You are a silly and petulant child who did not deserve the fame I lavished upon you. From this day forward you will *see* the souls that you deliver to me."

Norelle's eyes grew wide with horror. *No...it couldn't...I couldn't have!*

"Oh yes, Norelle, you have been collecting souls for me all this time and *you will continue to collect souls.* With each performance you give, while the crowd stands in ovation and you bask in the glow of fame untold, I will take their souls and they will never even know it...not until they die and come home to me.

Who would have thought - as music is *my* undoing *and yours* if I were to ever hear you sing - that your performances are the easiest way for me to gather souls? So many people...in one place. That is why I chose *you.* I could see the promise in you that others couldn't. The night I saw you on stage in that dive of a bar, I could not hear one word you sang...still...I knew.

Now, take my hand, or I can have you sing for the souls of the damned...the souls that *you* delivered to me...for all eternity."

Norelle broke down in sobbing despair. So *that* was why he wore earplugs at every performance she did! That was why they never listened to the radio and why he would not allow her to own a stereo! Even singing in the quiet of her bedroom netted her a terrific beating.

So much made sense now and it should have from long ago, but she was far too happy with her fame to question him or his motives. God had never done her any favors, so what else, *who else* did she have to turn to for her dream? She had no way of knowing that such immense fame would come with a price – a price that she *was not* willing to pay. *Why* should she have to pay anything for her gift? If she was born with it, it was hers, end of story!

She shook her head.

That kind of tenacity and that mode of strength had been her way of thinking in the early days of her career before she'd been broken by just how cruel God could be. She remembered one time telling a friend, one of the many she had before Franco came into her life, "He gives you a gift but you can't use it for money...you can only make a little here and there, instead having to rely on other work, meaningless and useless in the grand scheme of things, when others get whatever they want out of life."

She'd never understood why God singled *her* dreams out to destroy, but it really didn't matter. She had no loyalty to anyone any longer, except herself, but neither could she deny Franco. He was simply too powerful and she was simply too beaten down. All she wanted was a comfortable life, enough to live her dream; to pay her bills...to have clothes to wear and food to eat! *It's not fair,* her mind screamed!

She hesitantly reached her hand through the darkness and up to his and he grasped her wrist so hard that she heard the fragile bones in her wrist crack. She bit her lip to keep from

47

crying out. Franco would not tolerate her tears and she didn't wish to be beaten...*again*. She knew she had no choice.

Chapter Four
The Show Must Go On

Now she stood, as she always did, dreading another performance, dreading what she had to do, but the curtain had been raised and Franco pushed her out of the dressing room and into the wings.

"Now ladies and gentlemen...introducing what we have all been waiting for. The enchanting, the heavenly...the angel of light, Ms. Norelle Federiconi!"

The crowd erupted in wild cheers and an ovation greeted the lithe and beautiful woman as she stepped into the spotlight. The crowd sat down and the orchestra began playing, starting with her trademark "I am Your Spaniel" from Act One of "A Midsummer Night's Dream."

Norelle's rich soprano voice rang out as Helena, in love with Demetrius. The crowd sat, silent, entranced as she made the music come alive with her otherworldly strains.

As she always did, (but this time remembering Franco's words that she would *see exactly what she did for him*) she watched the crowd for the familiar wisps that taunted her at every performance. They weren't so noticeable at first, but then she could see them more clearly as they rose up from each person.

They circled slowly as if knowing that they were doomed and then drifted over to Franco who stood inconspicuously at the side exit door. He'd always occupied a spot by the side door and this time she could see that he was encased in a thick mist, his arms outstretched his mouth open and his eyes closed as he drank in each soul. No one paid any attention to him - everyone was far too engulfed in the worlds that Norelle took them to.

Why notice someone who would not garner a second look - when *she* was all that anyone could see? To the common observer, he too seemed to be totally enraptured by Norelle...a sight that truly was not uncommon.

She went right into her next aria, the role of Adriana Lecouvreur from Act One of the Italian opera "Io son l'umile ancella."

The crowd was silent...as silent as death as she sang. How sad that they did not even realize that they *were* dying...that by the time the performance was over, they would be dead - at least their souls would be - trapped, enslaved to a dark lord that showed no regret and no mercy.

As she finished, the crowd could contain its enthusiasm no longer and cheers abounded from deep within the audience.

She smiled through her tears and continued to her last performance of the evening as Agrippina from Act One of the Italian opera "L'alma mia fra le tempeste."

She sang her heart out as she watched the last of the souls from those unwitting victims fill Franco with the sustenance he wished for. She *would* be free this night, she could not, *would not* continue to damn people because they made the mistake of loving her voice and wishing to see her.

She bowed her head as the last words trailed from her lips. The room was silent for just a moment before the crowd roared with appreciation. The entire auditorium rose to their feet with shouts of "Brava" and roses fell at her feet on the dimly lit stage. She knelt and picked up a dark red rose, then a white one, then a yellow one. Holding them aloft, she slowly and gracefully curtsied. This would be a fitting way for her to go out, with the sounds of her adoring fans in her ears.

Chapter Five
Freedom...

"You did well tonight my dear Norelle. I am pleased."

Norelle nodded slowly. Franco sat down and closed his eyes for just a moment and that was all Norelle needed. She picked up the heavy angel statue that she brought to each performance and bashed Franco in the head as hard as she could. Franco never knew what hit him.

Chapter Six
The Cost...

"Oh Franco...Franco...wakey, wakey you gutter running rat!"

Franco's eyes snapped open and he tried to get up, but Norelle had secured him steadfastly to the chair with a roll of duct tape. Franco's ear plugs sat conspicuously in his lap.

Franco tried to speak but Norelle had saved the last piece of tape to silence the Devil's protests.

"Awww, what's the matter *Master*, shocked that you were so easily caught?"

Norelle huffed.

"I should have done this ages ago. What good is fame and fortune when your boss is the Devil?"

Norelle looked over at the angel statue. There had been a time when she believed in the power of angels. Now she believed in nothing. Life had caused her to be bitter and caustic and now she wished that life to be gone.

God had abandoned her; Satan asked too much and since she had abandoned one god, why should she replace it with another just as useless and hatefully cruel?

She needed no god, she needed only release and that was exactly what she'd have.

"Oh yes Franco, I will sing for you now. As you told me so long ago, music is your bane. I want to die and you will be coming with me."

She smiled.

"Besides, I wish to see for myself what my music will do to you. You were kind enough to show me what my music does *for* you, now I'd like to see what it will do *to* you. I owe you that much. At least I will be rid of you once and for all."

Franco's eyes grew wide with fear and he tried to wriggle free from his bonds, but he was helpless. As Norelle opened her mouth, she relished the fear and the look of pleading desperation that swallowed Franco's face.

"There was a time when men were kind, when their voices were soft and their words inviting..."

Franco's muffled squeals were awful, but Norelle sang, like she'd never sung before, she sang. Franco began to smoke and then his skin began melting from the bone. Norelle was both shocked and saddened by the demise of her captor. Like a candle melting after burning far too long, Franco seemed to simply burn away...his skin, followed by his internal organs dripping in small rivulets down his body and onto the floor. A puddle of blood and wasted, empty organs pooled at his feet as his body continued to liquefy from its foundation. Norelle began to feel weak but she continued to sing, her voice clear and strong.

"And the world was a song and the song was exciting. There was a time when it all went wrong...And still I dream he'll come to me, that we will live the years together...But there are dreams that cannot be and there are storms we cannot weather..."

With one final jerk of his frame, Franco's bloody skull snapped forward to the floor and rolled to Norelle's feet. She knelt down and with a frail hand, picked it up, clutching it as an actor would a prop. But she would never rise to her feet again.

On her knees, she cuddled the bloody skull, her voice breaking as her heart slowed...slowed...

"I had a dream my life would be so different from this hell I'm living, so different from what it seemed..."

As her vision darkened, the skull tumbled from her hands and her body fell with a dull thud to the floor.

"Now life has killed the dream...I dreamed..."

Josephine

How she fled in the night so cold and so gray
As she packed for travel far and away
Through the silver she stepped into a world unseen
Of a long ago place, to a land in between

On the shore the waves greeted her and sang her a rhyme
Stories of heroes and love so sublime
Maids danced in crystal and handsome men strolled
Animals pranced gaily so beautiful and bold

The mountaintops beckoned her to cliffs made of snow
How far they would take her, no one could know
None had returned from this journey so far
They'd step through the glass and wink out like a star

So up the mountain she strode, her purpose in mind
She sought not treasures but what her soul could find
The trek was long and fraught with care
But no matter the distance she was glad to be there

Her days became long as winter waved by
Spring rang her heart like a blue sapphire sky
In dreams she would visit me, I longed to see her heart
But fate had other plans and our link dashed apart

No longer in my mind by night nor by day
Her soul had fled freely, her spirit cast away
For fifty years now the story's been told
How much rings as true no one can know

I have watched as a sentry through the darkest of night
And awaited her voice at dawn's early light
She's rumored to still walk not in the land of the dead
But in that world in-between where "Farewell" is never said...

~**Epilogue**:~

I hope you've enjoyed these tales of ghostly romance,
the unusual and the eerie.

Some of these are pieces I wrote ***many***
years ago and some I wrote as recently as last
year.

It's been my pleasure to share my Darkness
with you...

~Author Bio:~

Andrea Dean Van Scoyoc is no stranger to the
Macabre, the Creepy and the Darkly Sinister.
A natural story-teller who can craft fanciful worlds
a reader really feels a part of, Andrea has no shortage
of, often shocking, imagination.

Andrea is also a musician, artist and filmmaker.

Please visit her official website to follow her on social media
and for FREE music, art, films and more...

https://linktr.ee/andreadeanhousedusk

www.ingramcontent.com/pod-product-compliance
Lightning Source LLC
Chambersburg PA
CBHW051459140726
47987CB00006B/2791